JESUS
IS
COMING AGAIN!

David R. Reagan

ILLUSTRATED BY PAULA LAWSON

JESUS IS COMING AGAIN

Copyright © 1992 by Harvest House Publishers
Eugene, Oregon 97402

Library of Congress Cataloging-in-Publication Data

Reagan, David, 1938-
      Jesus is coming again / David Reagan ; illustrated by Paula Lawson.
      Summary: Describes the Biblical prophecy of Jesus' return to earth, chronicling the events of the Rapture, Tribulation, Second Coming, Millennium, and Eternal State.
      ISBN 0-89081-989-0
      1. Second Advent—Juvenile literature.   2. Eschatology—Juvenile literature.   3. Bible—Prophecies—Juvenile literature.   [1. Second Advent.   2. Bible—Prophecies.]   I. Lawson, Paula, ill.   II. Title.
      BT886.R37   1992
      236′.9—dc20   92-3156
                                                                              CIP
                                                                              AC

Dedicated to

Jason, Reagan, Lauren and David

Jesus said: "There are many homes up there where my father lives, and I am going to prepare them for your coming. When everything is ready, then I will come and get you, so that you can always be where I am."

—*John 14:1-3*

When Jesus arose from the dead and went to Heaven, He left us with a promise. He said, "I will return."

Jesus is coming again !

Jesus will come first for His church. The church is made up of those who love Him.

A loud trumpet will sound, and Jesus will appear in the sky. Then, the dead Christians will rise up from their graves to meet Jesus in the sky. After that, the Christians who are alive will follow, rising through the air to meet Jesus in the sky.

This event is called the Rapture. All Christians, living and dead, will be taken off the earth.

The Rapture

A Great Miracle

When we meet the Lord in the sky, a great miracle will happen. Our bodies will be quickly changed.

First, our bodies will be made perfect. The blind will see, the deaf will hear, and the crippled will walk.

All diseases will be healed.

Second, our bodies will be made immortal. That means they will no longer grow old. We won't feel pain anymore. We will not get sick.

Our new bodies will be perfect, and they will last forever.

They will also be sinless. That means we won't do wrong things anymore. We will only want to do what is right.

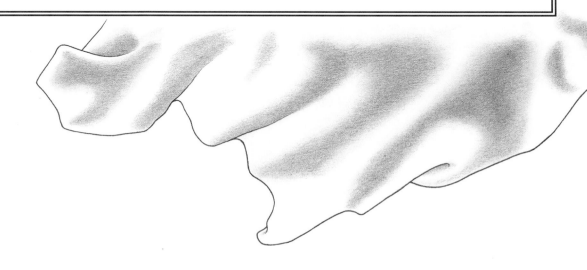

Our Judgement

After Jesus gives us our wonderful new bodies, we will be taken to Heaven with Him. Heaven is the beautiful place where God lives.

In Heaven, we will kneel before Jesus. Because we already believe in Him we will receive rewards. He will look at the record of our Christian life to see if we were kind to others. He will look to see if we obeyed our parents and teachers.

Some of us will receive beautiful robes to wear. Others will receive crowns.

The Great Feast

After all these rewards are handed out, Jesus will invite us to a great heavenly dinner. It will be the most wonderful feast in all of history. We will eat with Jesus and celebrate His saving us.

The Great Suffering

While we are happy in Heaven with Jesus, those people left on earth will be having a terrible time. They will suffer from war and hunger and disease, because they refused to believe in Jesus.

This suffering will cause some people to tell God they are sorry for the bad things they've done. Only when people admit that they've done wrong and turn to Jesus as their Savior can they be saved.

After seven years of this suffering, Jesus will return to this earth. He will bring with Him all of us who have been given new bodies. We will return with Jesus to the Mount of Olives outside the city of Jerusalem.

Jesus Returns Again

When we arrive with Jesus on that mountain, He will destroy all the enemies of God. The only ones who will be left alive will be those who gave their hearts to Jesus. Jesus will then begin to rule over all the earth from Jerusalem.

Jesus Rules !

Those of us in new bodies will be sent throughout the world to help Jesus rule over the earth.

Some of us will be judges. Some will serve as kings or presidents. Most of us will be teachers. We will teach the people about Jesus and explain how important it is to love Him.

During this time the world will be full of peace and joy. There won't be any war. Even the animals will live in peace together.

There won't be any poor people or people without homes. Every person will have enough to eat and will have a house to live in. People will be kind to each other.

This time of joy will last 1,000 years.

At the end of a thousand years, all the evil people who have ever lived will be raised from their graves. They will be judged and thrown into a place called Hell because they refused to love God and His Son, Jesus.

Hell is a sad place of suffering and separation from God. The Bible says it is a place of fire that burns forever.

Our New Home

But those that love Jesus will be taken to a beautiful new city that He is building now. It is called the New Jerusalem.

There is a house there especially for you. Other houses are prepared for everyone who loves Jesus.

From the New Jerusalem we will watch as God destroys the old earth with a great fire.

God will then make a new earth that will be perfect in every way. There won't be any harmful animals or plants.

There won't be any pollution in the air or in the water. There won't be any earthquakes or tornados or hurricanes. The new earth will be more beautiful than you can even imagine.

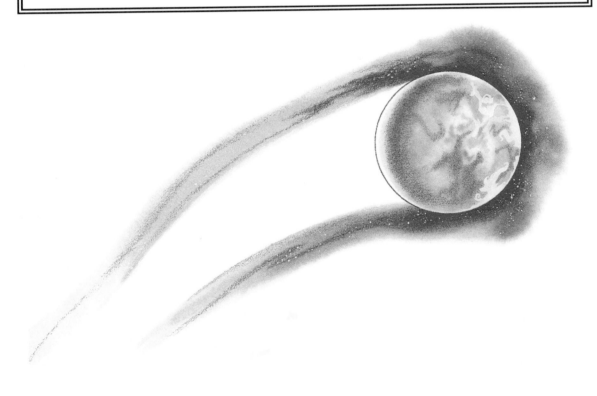

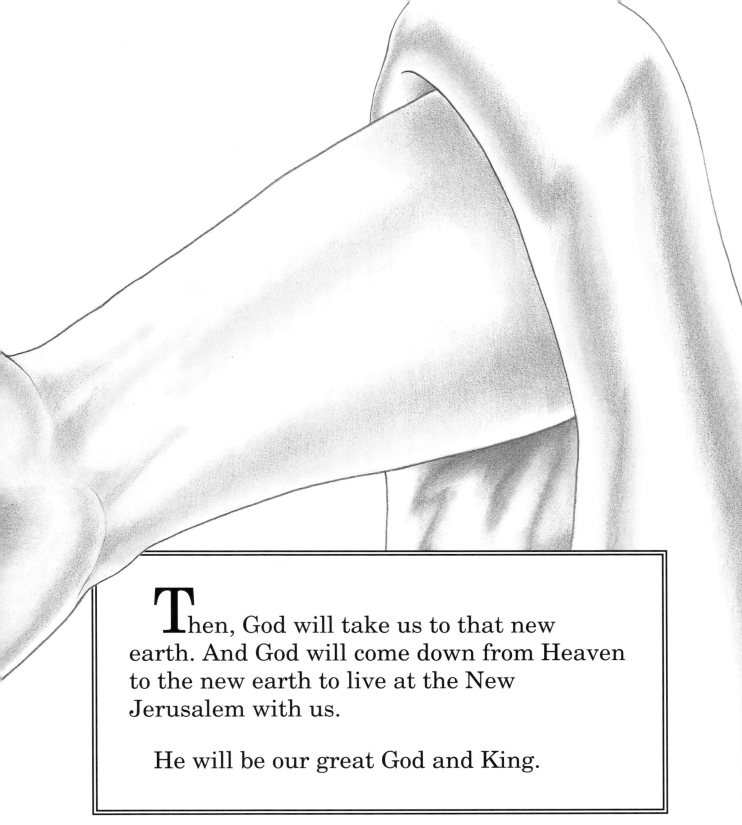

Then, God will take us to that new earth. And God will come down from Heaven to the new earth to live at the New Jerusalem with us.

He will be our great God and King.

Heaven on Earth

Eternity

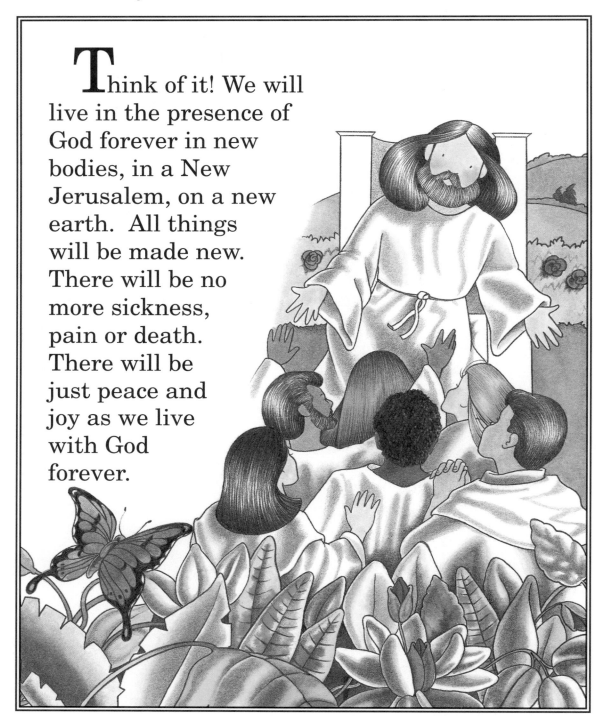

Think of it! We will live in the presence of God forever in new bodies, in a New Jerusalem, on a new earth. All things will be made new. There will be no more sickness, pain or death. There will be just peace and joy as we live with God forever.

Your Prayer

The Bible says that we are to pray, "Maranatha!" as we wait for the return of Jesus. Maranatha means, "Our Lord come!" Learn this new word and begin to use it in your prayers.

Jesus loves you, and He wants you to tell Him of your love for Him by praying, ***Maranatha!"***

When you use this word, it means you love Him and are excited about His return.

Scripture Notes for Parents

1) Page 1: The Promise - The last words Jesus spoke on the earth were spoken to the Apostle John on the island of Patmos about 65 years after the crucifixion and resurrection. Jesus promised John that He would return. See Revelation 22:20. (See also John 14:1-4 and Acts 1:9-11.)

2) Page 2: The Church - The Scriptures infer that the church will be taken out of the world before the Tribulation begins (I Thessalonians 1:10 and Luke 21:28)

4) Pages 2-3: The Rapture - This event is described in detail in I Thessalonians 4:13-18. (See also John 14:1-4.)

5) Pages 4-5: New Bodies - Paul teaches about the glorification of the believers' bodies in I Corinthians 15:42-44 & 51-55. (See also Philippians 3:20-21.)

6) Pages 6-7: Rewards - The Bible teaches that there will be degrees of rewards based upon our good works. See Matthew 11:20-24, Matthew 16:27, Luke 19:11-27, I Corinthians 4:5, II Corinthians 5:10, Revelation 19:8 and Revelation 22:12. We are not saved by works, but we are saved to do good works (Ephesians 2:8-10).

7) Page 7: Heaven - Jesus promises to take us to Heaven in John 14:1-4.

8) Pages 8-9: Banquet - The "marriage supper of the Lamb" is described in Revelation 19:7-9.

9) Pages 10-11: The Tribulation - Old Testament descriptions of this terrible period can be found in Isaiah 2:10-19, Jeremiah 30:4-7, Daniel 12:1, Joel 2:1-2 & Zephaniah 1:14-18. Jesus referred to this terrible period of time in Matthew 24:21 & 29. Paul described it in II Thessalonians 2:1-12. Chapters 6 through 19 of Revelation describe the events of the Tribulation in detail.

10) Pages 12-13: Jesus' Return - The return of Jesus to the Mt. of Olives is described in detail in Zechariah 14. It is also portrayed in Revelation 19:11-21.

11) Pages 14-15: The Millennium - The thousand year reign of Jesus is depicted in several graphic Old Testament passages. See Isaiah 2:1-4 and Micah 4:1-7. Also in Isaiah, see 24:21-23, 35:1-10 & 65:17-25. In the New Testament, the Lord's reign is described in Revelation 20.

12) Pages 16-17: Judgment & Hell - The judgment of the unrighteous is pictured in Revelation 20:11-15. In this passage Hell is referred to as a "lake of fire."

13) Pages 18-19: The New Jerusalem - This city is gloriously pictured in Revelation 21:10-23 and Revelation 22:1-5.

14) Page 19: The Fire - The destruction of the earth by fire is mentioned in II Peter 3:12-13.

15) Pages 20-21: The New Earth - Isaiah mentions the new earth in Isaiah 66:22. It is referred to again in Revelation 21:1. It will most likely be the present earth renovated by fire, for the Bible says the present earth is eternal (see Psalms 78:69 & 148:6).

16) Pages 22-24: Heaven on Earth - The coming to earth of God and the New Jerusalem is portrayed in Revelation 21:2-7. See also Revelation 22:1-5.

17) Page 25: "Maranatha!" - See I Corinthians 16:22 and Revelation 22:20.

Teaching Tips for Parents

A. To increase your children's comprehension of the story, you might follow up the reading of it by asking them the following questions:

1) What was the promise that Jesus left us with?
    Answer: "I will return." Note: You might find this promise in your child's Bible and underline it (Revelation 22:20).

2) What is the Rapture?
    Answer: The church being taken off the earth by Jesus.

3) Who will be raptured?
    Answer: Those who love Jesus.

4) Do you love Jesus?
    Discuss what it means to love someone. Talk about how the Bible teaches that those who love God obey Him (I John 5:3).

5) Did any part of the story make you sad?
    Possible answers: The people on earth who are left behind after the rapture to suffer. Or, the people sent to Hell. Note: Explain that their suffering is a result of their choice to refuse to love God.

6) What part of the story did you like best and why?

7) What does the word, Maranatha, mean?
    Answer: "Our Lord come!" Note: You might find this word in your child's Bible and underline it (I Corinthians 16:22).

B. Another thing you might do is ask your children to draw and color a picture to illustrate some scene from the story. An alternative would be to have them trace their favorite picture from the book and then color it. Ask them to add themselves to the picture. They can also color the picture on page 28 - or you can make copies of it for them to color.

C. If you sense that your child may be ready to receive Jesus as Savior, you might share the following points and scriptures;

1) All people are sinners — Romans 3:23.

2) All people need to be saved from their sins — Romans 6:23.

3) God has provided a way to save people from their sins — I Corinthians 15:3-4.

4) People cannot be saved in any other way except through Jesus — John 14:6.

5) What must a person do to be saved? — Acts 16:31.

If your child desires at this point to receive Jesus as Savior, then lead him or her in this prayer;

> "Dear Heavenly Father, I believe Your Son, Jesus, died for my sins. I am sorry for my sins. Please forgive me of them. I want to receive Your Son as my Savior from sin, and I want to become a member of Your family. Please send Jesus to live in my heart today. In Jesus' name, Amen."

Draw Yourself in this Picture